Awesome Animals ABC

www.kindermusik.com

ISBN 1-58987-095-6

Published in 2005 by Kindermusik International, Inc.

Library of Congress Cataloging-in-Publication Data

Biskup, Agnieszka.
  Awesome animals ABC / written by Agnieszka Biskup ; illustrated by David Brooks.
      p. cm.
  ISBN 1-58987-095-6 (hardcover)
  1. Animals—Juvenile literature. 2. English language—Alphabet—Juvenile literature.   I. Brooks, David, 1949- ill. II. Title.

QL49.B623 2005
590—dc22

                                                                                2005007804

Do-Re-Me & You! is a trademark of Kindermusik International, Inc.

Printed in China
First Printing, March 2005

Awesome Animals ABC

I am Fernando Flea.
I love animals.
All animals!

Me, up close!

written by
Agnieszka Biskup

illustrated by
David Brooks

A is for Ape

Big ears.
Cute baby.

Apes of all ages have amiable faces.
They look like us! (Though they live in different places.)

B is for Bee

No yellow stripes for me.
Basic black is fine.

A bee can bumble or buzz by the hour.
It's best at producing honey from flowers.

C is for Cat

Claws in when she creeps.
Claws out when she swipes.

The crafty cat creeps on silent paws,
Careful to pull in her sharp, curvy claws.

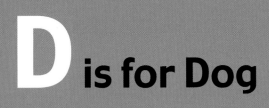

D is for Dog

Still has doggy breath.

DUKE

This daring dog has dozens of fans.
He sits and lies down and barks on command.

E is for Eel

Eats at night.
A real night-eel!

The elusive eel lives deep in the sea.
She's a fish—not a snake—so she swims easily.

F is for Frog

**The forest frog can be found on a log,
Until he l-e-e-a-a-p-s away—funny, long-legged frog!**

G is for Goose

Excellent swimmers.

Strong wings for long trips.

A goose likes to gather in a group called a gaggle.
When they all walk together, their tails wiggle-waggle.

H is for Hippopotamus

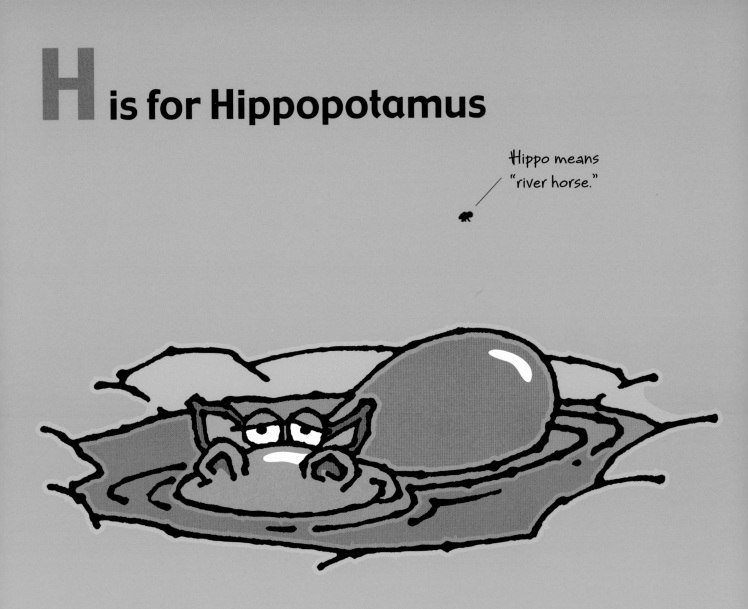

Hippo means "river horse."

Hello, hippo—you're huge!—from your hips to your head.
Let's hit the mud hole before we go to bed.

I is for Ibis

Likes marshy areas.

Ibis, oh, Ibis—are you really real?
Standing on one leg, you look so ideal!

J is for Jaguar

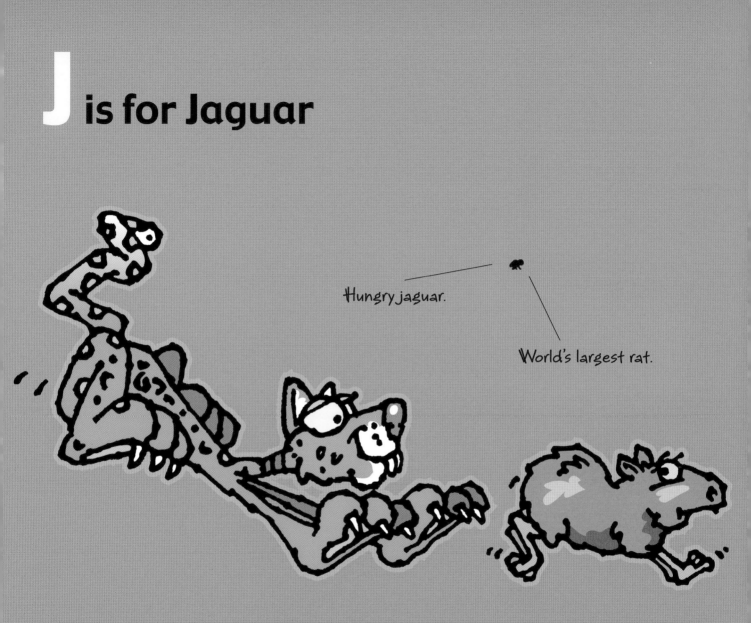

Hungry jaguar.

World's largest rat.

**The jaguar's just a jungle cat,
Who jumps to catch the jungle rat.**

K is for Kangaroo

He's a boomer. She's a flyer.
The baby is a joey. I'm a pest.

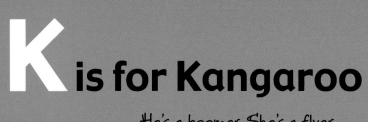

**Kangaroos jump—kangaroos have a pouch—
Kangaroos kick—that's a kangaroo ouch!**

L is for Llama

Thank you
for sharing.

A long-necked llama is likely to spit.
That mostly happens when he's frightened a bit.

M is for Mole

The mole is a mammal who moves underground,
Making tunnels in the dark, where more moles are found.

N is for Narwhal

Don't forget to floss.

A narwhal is a northern whale.
That horn? It's a tooth, and that's no tall tale!

O is for Okapi

Can clean its ears with its tongue.

**Okapi bounds over the open plain.
Okay, Okapi—off you go again!**

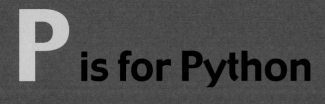

P is for Python

Scaly skin.

The powerful python squeezes its prey.
It hugs so tight, people stay far away!

Likes to hang out in a group called a covey.

**This quaint little bird is a bobwhite quail.
He calls "bob white" on a quiet country trail.**

R is for Rat

I get kicked out of
houses a lot, too.

A rat is a rodent resembling a mouse.
Unless he's a pet, he's kicked out of the house.

S is for Salmon

Young salmon are called fry. Get it—small fry!

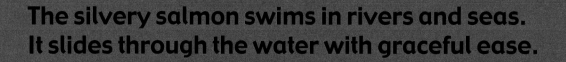

**The silvery salmon swims in rivers and seas.
It slides through the water with graceful ease.**

T is for Tarantula

Big—but not poisonous.

The tarantula is so terribly hairy—
Not too tiny—and terrifically scary.

U is for Unicorn

Have you met the narwhal? I think you two would get along.

Unicorns usually show up in books.
They're uniquely magic—with uniquely good looks.

V is for Vampire Bat

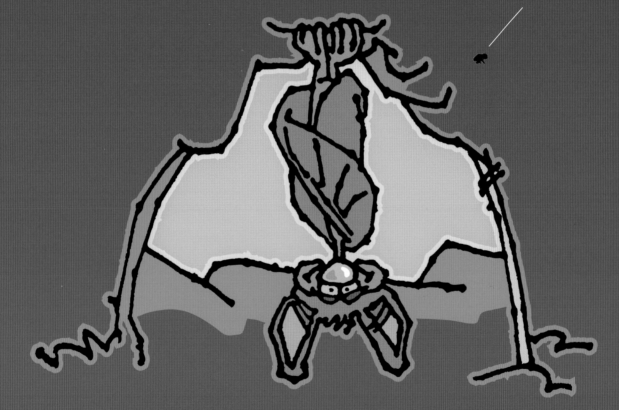

Sleeps in the day.
Eats at night.

The vampire bat varooms through the air,
Then naps in a cave. What's the view like in there?

W is for Worm

Hard to tell their heads from their tails.

It's a wonderful day for a wiggly worm,
Warm and wet—just watch the worm squirm!

X is for X-ing

Where's the "Flea X-ing" sign?

No animal starts with the letter "X."
But you've all seen animals X-ing, I'll bet!

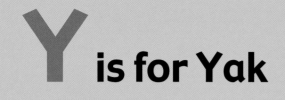

Y is for Yak

These guys love
the mountains.

Yikkity, yakkity, a young yak yaks,
With a yoke on its neck or a pack on its back.

Z is for Zebra

They don't fool me.

The zoo's new zebras can be hard to spot—
Their zig-zag stripes blend in such a lot.